# SENSITIVE GUYS

by MJ Kaufman

at www.trwplays.com and www.trwplays.co.uk. Inquiries concerning all other rights should be forwarded on to

TRW Plays
A division of Theatrical Rights Worldwide
1180 Avenue of the Americas, 6th Floor
New York, NY 10036
trwplays@theatricalrights.com

and

TRW Plays
A division of Theatrical Rights Worldwide
122-124 Regent Street
London W1B 5SA UK
trwplays@theatricalrights.co.uk

Printed in the U.S.A. / U.K.
ISBN: 978-1-63852-017-7

# WHO

*(all the characters are played by people who identify as women, nonbinary, or gender non-conforming)*

Men's Peer Education Group

**DANNY:** Facilitator. Founder. Senior. White. Upper middle class.
**TYLER:** Co-Facilitator. Founder. Senior. Black. Middle class.
**JORDAN:** Senior. White. Well-off.
**PETE:** Sophomore. Working class. Latino and/or Asian-American.
**WILL:** New guy. Freshman. Working class. White.

DANNY is double-cast with DIANA
TYLER is double-cast with TRACY
JORDAN is double-cast with KATIE
PETE is double-cast with AMY
WILL is double-cast with LESLIE

Survivor Support Group

**DIANA:** President. Founder. Upper-middle-class.
**TRACY:** Co-President and founder. Working class.
**KATIE:** Vice President. Working class.
**AMY:** Secretary. Well-off.
**LESLIE:** New girl. Working class.

ALSO the adults:

**ADMISSIONS OFFICER:** played by the person playing LESLIE/WILL

**DEAN**: played by the person playing AMY/PETE
**JONES**: played by the person playing KATIE/JORDAN


## WHERE

Watson College. A small liberal arts college. A classroom where student meetings happen. It smells like glue and sharpies. There are some radical posters on the walls and books on the shelves. Also various offices.


## WHEN

Spring semester.


## SYNOPSIS

The Men's Peer Education group at Watson College is dedicated to unpacking and exposing male privilege. These "sensitive guys" believe that through increased self-awareness they can end sexual violence on campus; but when a shocking rumor surfaces, the group is shaken to the core. *Sensitive Guys* features a cast of women and gender nonconforming actors, double-cast as male and female characters, who try to understand men who are trying to understand masculinity.


## PUNCTUATION

A / means the following line overlaps starting at the slash.

# Scene One

*The classroom.*

*Admissions officer stands before the audience.*

*They show a projected image of a dead white guy.*

**ADMISSIONS OFFICER:**
This is James Watson. Founder of our college. Military
man. Grew up fighting in the Union Army. Battle
of Gettysburg. A courageous fellow, he stayed in the
fight even when it wasn't easy. He wrote letters home
to his dear wife Mary about how much he dreamed
of founding a school for her to teach in. She was a
history teacher who taught illiterate children in one-
room schoolhouses covered by snow. Her dream was to
start a college where the children could learn in peace,
unhampered by the difficulties of rural life. And so
James suffered through the long war. And all the
while he wrote letters home to Mary. And when he
finally got home he used everything he had to found
a college for her to teach in. Right here. I'm sure it's
clear to you that this is no ordinary school. Watson
is... unparalleled. This is a place where people take

action. Where dreams are realized, just as James Watson realized Mary's dream. I invite you to realize your dreams at Watson College.

# Scene Two

*The classroom.*

*Survivor support group.*

*DIANA, TRACY, KATIE, AMY.*

**DIANA:**
Hi Everyone.

**TRACY:**
Thanks for coming to our presentation.

**KATIE:**
Thanks so much.

**AMY:**
And welcome!

**KATIE:**
Yes indeedy!

>　　　*DIANA shoots her a look.*

**DIANA:**
Are you gonna do it like that?

**KATIE:**
I'm not gonna do it like that.

**DIANA:**
Good.

**TRACY:**
So.

**AMY:**
We are SECTS!

**DIANA:**
Sex?

**AMY:**
SECTS.
Students Empowered to Confront and Transform Sexism

**DIANA:**
Um when did we come up with that?

**AMY:**
I came up with it. Clever right?

**KATIE:**
I was happy with Student Coalition to Confront Sexual Assault

**AMY:**
That had zero acronym potential
I mean SCCSA?

**KATIE:**
Yeah but calling ourselves SECTS feels a little

*She makes a face*

**DIANA:**
Keep going.

**TRACY:**

Great. So we are the Survivor Support Group and we work with the Men's Peer Education group on three things.

**DIANA:**

And then you'll hit go on the projector[1]

**TRACY:**

And then I'll hit go on the projector

**DIANA:**

And then you'll say

**TRACY:**

And then I'll say
Confronting,
Preventing,
and Eradicating
sexual assault on Watson's campus and beyond.

**AMY:**

Within the next five years.

**DIANA:**

Let's not share that part publicly.

**KATIE:**

But that's true.

**TRACY:**

Don't you think it will seem a little cocky?

**DIANA:**

Essentially unrealistic?

---

[1] For virtual productions this line can be changed to "DIANA: And then you'll start our presentation… TRACY: And then I'll start our presentation"

**TRACY:**

We're not superheroes! Not yet!

**KATIE:**

But we are actually making a plan to do that.

**DIANA:**

But we want them to take us seriously.

**AMY:**

Let's practice the part about transformative justice, it's really good and you guys haven't gotten to see it yet

**KATIE:**

Sure. So. We use a transformative justice framework. That means we believe that in order to eradicate sexual assault we are going to have to transform society. Our current system AKA the criminal justice system—

**AMY:**

AKA the NO JUSTICE EVER system!

**KATIE:**

Amy.

**AMY:**

Sorry.

**KATIE:**

That system views perpetrators of sexual assault as CRIMINALS! Scary! And responds to acts of sexual violence by punishing the perpetrator and removing them from society.
Ahhem.

> *AMY pulls on a police hat and changes up her swagger.*

**AMY:**

You sir, have been convicted of rape. And we're going to throw you in prison. For a long, long time!

**DIANA:**

Oh my god.

**KATIE:**

We found this response to be insufficient because punishment and isolation so far has failed to end sexual assault.

**AMY (as policeman):**

Another day, another rapist in jail.

**KATIE:**

And also because removing the perpetrators means they can go on to commit sexual assault elsewhere.

**AMY (as policeman):**

Sir, you gotta cut that out—no rape allowed in prison either!

**DIANA:**

Okay no.

**TRACY:**

Just let them.

**KATIE:**

AND MOST IMPORTANTLY it doesn't address what we have come to believe are the ROOT CAUSES of sexual violence, which is just mostly

**KATIE and AMY:**

The Big Bad PATRIARCHY.

**DIANA:**

The policeman character is offensive.

**AMY:**

It's funny.

**KATIE:**

That wasn't the end.

**DIANA:**

Police and prisons are real things in people's lives—it's a fucked system, we shouldn't laugh at it.

**KATIE:**

Our presentation makes you wanna jump off a building. We have to lighten the edge.

**TRACY:**

We just need to practice more and get better at not interrupting each other.

**AMY:**

I'm concerned about how long it's taking us to get to the meat of the thing.

**DIANA:**

I hate it when you use that metaphor. Meat.

**KATIE:**

A spoonful of sugar helps the medicine go down.

**TRACY:**

I think we have the perfect mix of humor and real talk.

**DIANA:**

People need to be able to take the raw truth of what we're doing.

**KATIE:**

I just wonder how effective that is as a strategy.

**AMY:**

You know how many members the Environmental Student Action group has? Or the women's history month coalition? OMG the Students Transforming and Resisting Corporations? They're so big now they're meeting in South View.

**TRACY:**

Seriously? South View?

**DIANA:**

What we do isn't glamorous. It's not for everyone. You have to really believe in shit to show up to our meetings. We're not just like a resume booster for the wanna-be non-profit executives.

**AMY:**

But we want people to actually SHOW UP.

**DIANA:**

Well that's what this presentation is for! If we ever finish it.

**KATIE:**

I thought it was for the administration. Like if we don't do it they're gonna take away our group status or something.

**DIANA:**

Well yeah it's dual purpose.

**AMY:**

What do you mean take away our group status?

**TRACY:**

They uh they said that in order to keep getting funding and reserving a room and all that we have to make a presentation for prospective students' weekend.

**DIANA:**

Something about "giving back" to the community.

**AMY:**

Seriously?  Just us or other groups too?

**KATIE:**

Just us.

**DIANA:**

They don't really believe we're doing anything? Maybe?

**AMY:**

I thought it was just to get new members.

**TRACY:**

I mean it would be great if new people joined cuz of it.

**KATIE:**

*(to DIANA)* Maybe you could write a song for it. That would be a nice change of pace.

**TRACY:**

Um.  I mean I love Di's music but it's not exactly...

**AMY:**

Uh yeah.

**KATIE:**

What?

**DIANA:**

I only write riot grrl angry feminist songs. You know that.

**KATIE:**

You had that one kind of quiet sweet one.

**DIANA:**

About all the men in the world dying?

**TRACY:**

Again I LOVE your work, Di I just don't think it's—
right for/what we wanna—

**AMY:**

Yeah no.

**DIANA:**

I'm not really willing to dumb down my voice for this.

**KATIE:**

Ok. Yeah. Bad idea. Sorry.

**AMY:**

Oh shit. I was supposed to be at my work-study job ten
minutes ago.

**KATIE:**

I thought you never get penalized for lateness.

**AMY:**

Well I can't be like late late.

**KATIE:**

What's late late?

**AMY:**

I don't know like fifteen minutes?

**TRACY:**

It sounds like our meeting's over.

**KATIE:**

That is what it sounds like.
I guess we'll... come back to this?

**DIANA:**

Our presentation is in three weeks.

**KATIE:**

I think we're gonna do great.  What?
I know we are.

*She puts out her hand.*

C'mon.
Oh we ALWAYS—
YES TODAY TOO!

*DIANA, AMY and TRACY put their hands out.*

**ALL TOGETHER**

Three...two...one...JUSTICE!!

# Scene Three

*They become college-age cis-guys.*

*Somewhere between boys and men.*

*They are now DANNY, TYLER, JORDAN, PETE.*

*The Men's Peer Education Group.*

*WILL enters.*

*It's his first meeting.*

**DANNY:**
We talk one at a time.

**PETE:**
That's important.

**DANNY:**
We're demonstrating right now.

**PETE:**
Sort of.

**TYLER:**
We speak from I. So if you find yourself about to say

something that starts with the words "all men," try to reframe and speak from "I."

**JORDAN:**

Step forward step back.

**DANNY:**

Move.

**JORDAN:**

That's right. Move Forward, Move Back. Step is ableist cuz not everyone steps. Anyways, it means that if you're the kind of person that's usually first to answer a question you're supposed to hang back and let other people talk. And if you're the kind of person that's afraid to talk in public you should take a chance and talk first.

**PETE:**

Confidentiality. Okay so that's pretty self-explanatory. What's said here stays here what's learned here leaves here. Cute, right?

**TYLER:**

If someone says something mind-blowing by all means take the idea with you. Just avoid being like 'Pete in my Unlearning Male Privilege Group said this'. Because that would give away that Pete is in the group and he might not want that.

**DANNY:**

We're not called that anymore.
Now it's Men's Peer Education Group.

**TYLER:**

Much like our identities our group name is a constant work in progress.

**DANNY:**

And I don't know if we've said it officially but welcome!

**TYLER:**

Welcome!

**PETE:**

Yeah, man!

**JORDAN:**

We're very happy to have you.

**DANNY:**

Maybe you could tell us a bit about yourself.

**TYLER:**

You can really get into it. Tell us how you got here and all that.

**WILL:**

I'm William Donald Warner. The third.

**PETE:**

That's a lotta name, man.

**JORDAN:**

What dorm are you in?

**WILL:**

I actually don't live on campus. I live with my grandmother on Green Street.

**PETE:**

Cool, cool. That's great, man.

**WILL:**

I like soccer. I wanna be an engineer.

**DANNY:**

Tell us more about what brought you to this group.

**WILL:**

My grandmother. She wants me to be better.
I took Introduction to Feminism last semester.
Her idea.

**JORDAN:**

How'd you like it?

**WILL:**

To be honest I just did it to meet girls. But then I
liked the class. It was a lot of talking and sharing.
And that never happens in my other classes. I wanted
to take another women's studies class but I didn't have
room in my schedule. So I'm doing this instead.

**TYLER:**

Nice.

**DANNY:**

Well, we're glad you're here!

**PETE:**

Welcome, man!

**JORDAN:**

Glad to have ya!

**DANNY:**

You ready to take it away Jordan?

**JORDAN**

Sure sure.
So. You're at a party.
It's late at night.
You see a drunk boy slip something into a drunk girl's
drink.
I mean woman, drunk woman.

What do you do?
Remember the goal is to keep her from leaving with him.

**TYLER:**
Do you know the woman?

**JORDAN:**
Let's say no.

**PETE:**
Like don't even know her name?

**JORDAN:**
Let's say you know her a little bit.
You have a class with her or something.

**DANNY:**
That's more than a little bit.

**JORDAN:**
Well okay that's how much you know her.

**TYLER:**
You could know her a lot just from one class.

**JORDAN:**
Well you don't. You've seen her around. You know her name.
That's it. It's a big class. Econ one let's say.

**PETE:**
I got this.

**JORDAN:**
Yeah Pete!

**DANNY:**
Whatcha got?

**PETE:**

Okay, you grab the guy by the shoulders football bro style and are like, hey man I got this super sweet weed off a buddy with a hookup come smoke a quick splif with me! And while you're distracting him your other pal comes along and gives the girl a little heads-up, telling her not to consume said drink.

**DANNY:**

My only question is what if this guy puts up a fight?

**PETE:**

Well then you back off.

**DANNY:**

What happens to the woman if he puts up a fight?

**PETE:**

I don't know you find another way to tell her.

**DANNY:**

And what's that other way?

**PETE:**

I don't know man make it up, I already made one up.

**WILL:**

What does she expect from hanging out with douche-bags like that in the first place?

**JORDAN:**

Uh no, man.

**PETE:**

We don't do that.

**WILL:**

Don't do what?

**JORDAN:**
What you just did.

**WILL:**
What did I just do?

**TYLER:**
It's called victim-blaming.

**DANNY:**
It's never their fault.

**WILL:**
'Cept when it is.

**DANNY:**
It never is.

**WILL:**
Hanging out with certain people? That's just asking for it.

**PETE**
Oh Will Man.

**JORDAN:**
I'm so glad you're here with us.

**TYLER:**
So am I.

**DANNY:**
Me too.

**WILL:**
W-what's going on?

**JORDAN:**
Let's play it out this way. If you were walking down the street and someone shot you would that be your

fault for walking in the wrong place or wearing the wrong clothes /or having the wrong hairstyle?

**WILL:**

Depends where I was walking. I mean if I was up in Northside then I'm prolly just asking for it. Sketchy as hell up there.

**TYLER:**

You mean black people live there?

**WILL:**

I mean there's definitely more crime up there.

**DANNY:**

Okay, so this is the thing. It doesn't depend on anything. No matter how a victim is behaving they don't deserve abuse. No matter where anyone lives or what they look like, they don't deserve harm. No one deserves abuse or violence. The one responsible is the one who perpetrated harm.

**JORDAN:**

And aren't we supposed to say survivor?

**DANNY:**

I mean like if it's between the victim and the perpetrator./I mean the person who perpetrated harm.

**PETE:**

What about someone who is both a victim and a perpetrator?

**DANNY:**

/That's not what we're talking about right now.

**PETE:**

That's not uncommon. Especially in jails. People are

victims and perpetrators. /Cycles of violence.

**TYLER:**
Guys. Guys. Guys. Women should be able to act and dress and hang out with whoever they want without risking being abused for it! That's all we're trying to say!

**DANNY:**
That one might take some time to absorb.

**TYLER:**
It's a really great conversation.

**JORDAN:**
Yes, thanks Will for bringing it up.

**PETE:**
So glad you're with us.

> *They all cheer for WILL.*

> *They jump up and pat him on the back.*

> *A ritual: like he just scored a goal on the football field.*

> *WILL steps back.*

**WILL:**
What's like the trick?
To being a good guy?

**JORDAN:**
Good question, Will.

**DANNY:**
The quintessential question to be exact.

**PETE:**

I'm so glad we can have these conversations.

**JORDAN:**

Amen.

**WILL:**

No but really though, how do you do it?
How do you become a good man?

*The others look at him and exchange a knowing glance.*

**DANNY:**

What you'll see if you continue to return to meetings is that this stuff is not fast food.

**JORDAN:**

Everyone's gonna have their own process for unlearning.

**PETE:**

You say that man but shit's hard-wired.

**JORDAN:**

No one's denying that it's a long road. But look how far you've come! In just a short time, man!

**PETE:**

You really think so?

**JORDAN:**

Hundred percent. Like what happened the other day when we were chilling?

**DANNY:**

When exactly were you chilling?

**JORDAN:**

Oh we were like chilling the other day.

**DANNY:**
What day?

**JORDAN:**
Tuesday, I think.
Was it Tuesday?

**PETE:**
Yeah Tuesday.

**DANNY:**
Well, what happened?

**PETE:**
It was just. We were hanging out with some girls.

**DANNY and TYLER and JORDAN:**
Women.

**PETE:**
I mean, women. We were hanging out with some women. And we were like talking and eating pizza and shit.

**DANNY:**
What women?

**PETE:**
Katie and Tracy.

**TYLER:**
Confidentiality?

**PETE:**
Too late! Sorry man.
And Tracy was like telling a whole angry feminist rant like she does.

**JORDAN:**
Dude.

**PETE:**
What?

**JORDAN:**
Watch how you—

**PETE:**
Wait are you guys dating?

**JORDAN:**
You shouldn't be calling anyone an angry feminist.

**PETE:**
But that's what she calls herself.

**TYLER:**
It's different when you say it.

**PETE:**
I'm not saying it like a bad thing.

**JORDAN:**
Whatever. Never mind. It's like a stereotype about black women.  That they're all angry.

**PETE:**
I respect your girlfriend, man.

**JORDAN:**
We're not—

**DANNY:**
Maybe you should just finish the story.

**PETE:**
Sure. Okay.  So what happened was. Basically. I didn't interrupt her.

**JORDAN:**
It was a bigger deal than that.

**PETE:**
It was the thing we always talk about.
Raising your voice to take over a room.

**DANNY:**
*(To WILL)* That's a thing we talk about.
How men command power in a room.

**JORDAN:**
It was textbook. Here's Tracy mid-feminist rant and
Pete looks up and says something like "no way" and—

**PETE:**
Hell the fuck no. Is what I said.
She was talking about okay
I don't think I can bring it up here what she was
talking about.

**TYLER:**
That's good. Respecting confidentiality.

**PETE:**
No it's not because of confidentiality it's because it was
gross as hell.

**JORDAN:**
To you.

**PETE:**
To you too, man, don't lie.

**WILL:**
What was she talking about?

**JORDAN:**
It's a little bit hard to describe.

**PETE:**
It's like this. When girls /get their

**DANNY and TYLER and JORDAN:**
WOMEN

**PETE:**
When women get their periods. There's some women that don't uh put anything up there. They just—what did she call it?

**JORDAN:**
Free bleeding.

**PETE:**
Yup. That. I don't really want to say it.
But they do that. All over their clothes.
And everything and everyone else.
It's supposed to be
Empowering.

**WILL:**
Wow.

**PETE:**
That was exactly my reaction.
Or actually my exact reaction was
HELL THE FUCK NO.

**JORDAN:**
He shouted it across the room.

**PETE:**
I really did.

**JORDAN:**
It was like everything we talk about in here.
All heads turned toward him.
Everyone was like waiting for him to launch into something. I mean Tracy was mid-sentence but you could

tell everyone was gonna listen to him but he didn't/
continue.

**PETE:**

How about I tell what I didn't do?

**JORDAN:**

Sure.

**PETE:**

I said, excuse me.  Please continue.

**DANNY:**

Damn.

**JORDAN:**

And she did.

**DANNY:**

And people listened to her?

**PETE:**

Oh yeah.

**DANNY:**

Hey man.  That's awesome.
You're using what you practice. In here.
I'm proud of you.

**PETE:**

Thanks, man.

**TYLER:**

Way to integrate.

**DANNY:**

Should we finish off on that note?

**TYLER:**

Sounds about right.

**DANNY:**
Will, just do what we do.

*They circle up. They put their hands in the circle.*

**ALL OF THEM TOGETHER**
We vow to confront the barbarism of human beings.
We vow to challenge oppression in all its forms.
We transform our selves and in doing so
Transform the world.

# Scene Four

*LESLIE and DEAN.*

**LESLIE:**
I can't focus in class.

**DEAN:**
Okay.
What class?

**LESLIE:**
American History 19th century focus.

**DEAN:**
AMAZING era. Really changed my life when I studied the history of our country. Who's the professor?

**LESLIE:**
Anderson.

**DEAN:**
Uh huh one of our finest don't you just love her?

**LESLIE:**
Actually I /really do

**DEAN:**
And she's gotten that teaching award three years in a

row. Did you read her new book that just came out?

**LESLIE:**
Yeah it's actually—

**DEAN:**
What was it the Ass and the Man or the Man and the Ass?

**LESLIE:**
The Man the Ass and the Machine.

**DEAN:**
About the industrial revolution and agriculture!

**LESLIE:**
Yeah I wrote a paper on it in high school.
She was one of the reasons I chose Watson.

**DEAN:**
Isn't that phenomenal. What you kids are getting here is an absolutely first-class education. It is just wonderful that you get to spend—how many hours a week is it? 2 or 3?

**LESLIE:**
Uh two and half.

**DEAN:**
With one of the world's leading scholars of American History.
Isn't that incredible?

**LESLIE:**
Yes it is but I
I'm coming to see you because
I actually can't focus in class.

**DEAN:**

Right right!

I'm so glad you came to me!

And why is that again?

**LESLIE:**

Well because of this boy

this other student.

**DEAN:**

Okay yes tell me.

**LESLIE:**

We had a thing.

We um.

Something happened with us and it's...

Hard to see him in class.

Hard for me to focus.

**DEAN:**

Can you tell me more specifically?

**LESLIE:**

Like my hands start shaking when I see him and uh

sometimes I start to uh I start to cry and—

**DEAN:**

Well this sounds very rough.

Can you tell me more about what happened with the

boy?

**LESLIE:**

It was um

It was like

He did something we were uh

It was we were um together alone and he uh

We were it was supposed to be uh

It was supposed to be something different
it was
it was too much

**DEAN:**

I see. I have to stop you now. I have to tell you that you that I'm a mandatory reporter. If you tell me that someone hurt or assaulted you, I'm required to report it. Or else I could lose my job. I have to let you know that before you tell me anything else. I'm not sure if you want this reported.

**LESLIE:**

I don't. I just don't want to see him in class.

**DEAN:**

I see. I see. So this boy is a problem for you.

**LESLIE:**

Yes.

**DEAN:**

Yes well I could certainly switch you out.

**LESLIE:**

Oh no I mean I want to keep the class.
It's um actually well.
I was actually wondering if we could switch him out.

**DEAN:**

I see. It's not particularly appropriate to switch out a student for no reason.

**LESLIE:**

Well I don't really want to like discuss it with him. I um. I don't really ever wanna see him again.

**DEAN:**

This incident seems to have caused a great deal of stress.

**LESLIE:**

It yeah my semester really uh fell apart since.

**DEAN:**

I'm so sorry to hear that. Have you visited the counseling center?

**LESLIE:**

I... no. I'm not looking for that right now.

**DEAN:**

Okay... I also wonder if you might consider taking some time off.

**LESLIE:**

From school?

**DEAN:**

It sounds like you're really having a hard time here.

**LESLIE:**

Well I mean I can keep it together.

**DEAN:**

We want you to excel here. To really do your best.

**LESLIE:**

I don't know if I can take time off. I want to graduate with my class.

**DEAN:**

Well it's something for you to think about.

**LESLIE:**

I'm just wondering about

Um
Because
You know
What he did to me
It wasn't like
It really
I was wondering about
Him getting kicked out of the class?
Not me
And like I came here to study with Anderson
I came here to take her class
So I don't really want to drop out of it
And I don't want to do poorly in it

**DEAN:**

Okay okay
This has really been an ordeal hasn't it?
I can really understand not wanting to miss a semester
or class you really care about. I will say that having
seen other students in similar states of turmoil—taking
some time is actually quite important. You can't really
do your best right now. You need to rest. To really sit
with what happened, to heal, to think through everyone's role in everything. It sounds like it's still a little
unclear to you what exactly happened.

**LESLIE:**

I no I don't think unclear I just um it's hard to talk
about.
Assault is hard to talk about

**DEAN:**

So a few minutes ago when you were talking about it
you sounded a little more confused. You didn't use that
word.

*Sensitive Guys*

**LESLIE:**

I ok I don't remember exactly what I said I just I know
that what he did to me wasn't
it wasn't okay

**DEAN:**

These are serious words you are throwing around here
and they need to be considered with care. If you want
to file a complaint against a student you need to really
be sure about what we're talking about. You need to
really have your story straight. So I need you to take
some time. Think through what happened and think
through whether or not you actually need to do anything about it. Again, I'll say a semester off has been
very transformative for other students. I want you to
succeed here at Watson. So I need you to give yourself
the time and space to recover.

# Scene Five

*Survivor Support Group.*

*Classroom from before.*

*DIANA, TRACY, KATIE, AMY.*

**TRACY:**
He was on the edge of his seat. He was so uncomfortable. He shouted out "Hell the fuck no," and then realized what he had done and tried to swallow whatever it was that wanted to come tumbling out? It was so awkward. Like you could see him kinda writhing with pain?

**KATIE:**
Well I mean he was pretty uncomfortable.

**AMY:**
Not talking makes guys SO uncomfortable.

**TRACY:**
I wish he had talked. I wish he had voiced whatever idiotic ideas about free bleeding he had come up with. Especially because I would not have LET him take the power, obvi.

**DIANA:**

Funny how they think they have all the power.

**KATIE:**

They do not think they have all the power.

**DIANA:**

That is legit what they talk about at their meetings. They think they have all the power in every room. When they open their mouths everyone MUST just want to listen to them.

**TRACY:**

And every moment that they cede to a woman is worth extensive pats on the back.

**KATIE:**

Do you say these things around your boyfriend?

**AMY:**

Love isn't like that.

**KATIE:**

Isn't like what?

**AMY:**

Beyond criticism.

**TRACY:**

Jordan's great but he's working on his shit same as anyone else.

*LESLIE enters. She listens outside the door.*

**DIANA:**

Jordan is exceptional, real exceptional as far as men go. But he's a man. And he's never going to get over being a man. It's like being a dog. A dog can be special. A dog can be incredible, can literally save your life, but it will never be able to do the things that humans can do. Because it is not a human. It is a dog.

**TRACY:**
Wow, Di.

**AMY:**
Bet you don't share THAT metaphor with Jordan.

**KATIE:**
I don't want to be difficult but like.
If a dog can never stop being a dog?
If a man can never stop being a man?
Isn't the whole thing we're doing here CALLED transformative?
That's like the deal, right?
Transformative justice?
We transform ourselves to transform society?

**DIANA:**
I'm not saying they can't change.

**TRACY:**
That is sort of exactly what you just said.

**AMY:**
Guys don't you think we should practice the presentation? Two weeks away?

**KATIE:**
Great point. Who wants to kick us off?

*Everyone groans.*

*LESLIE knocks on the door.*

*They all turn to look at her.*

**LESLIE:**

Is this uh survivor support group?

**KATIE:**

Yes!

**TRACY:**

Welcome!

**AMY:**

Come in!

**LESLIE:**

Is it uh open hour? Like for new members?

**TRACY:**

Absolutely. We were just taking care of some core group business while we waited for the new members to arrive.

**DIANA:**

Sorry we didn't notice you.

**AMY:**

No one comes to open hour.

**KATIE:**

Sometimes people come!

**AMY:**

No one's come in like

**TRACY:**

Maybe we should orient our new member

**KATIE:**

Sure!

**AMY:**

Orient how?

**TRACY:**

Well we're Survivor Support Group! I'm Tracy, co-president.

**DIANA:**

Diana, other co-president.

**KATIE:**

Katie, vice-president.

**AMY:**

Amy. Secretary.

**LESLIE:**

Leslie.

**TRACY:**

Should we go over our approach?
Survivor-centered?

**KATIE:**

I think that's a good idea.
We haven't gone over that in a while.

**AMY:**

We go over that every meeting.

**DIANA:**

Ahhm, we use a survivor-centered approach. Which means we support survivors no matter what. That's the whole purpose of our group. So in the aftermath of an assault we do whatever the survivor wants. If they want to report it to campus police, we do. If they want to report it to police police we do. If she—I mean they—want to file a lawsuit we do it. If they want to have a touchy-feely mediation meeting with the abuser we do it. You can tell how I feel about those.

**TRACY:**

Di.

**DIANA:**

Some people like that.

**KATIE:**

Anyway, we're so glad you're here!

**TRACY:**

Any questions?

**LESLIE:**

What I tell you, what happens to it?

**KATIE:**

It gets recorded.

**DIANA:**

We like to have a record of every incident.

**TRACY:**

Depending on what you want we can report it. Survivor centered.

**LESLIE:**

Okay.

Okay. Just like that?

**TRACY:**

Just like what?

**LESLIE:**

I tell you what happened?

**TRACY:**

Whatever you want to talk about.

**KATIE:**

Do you need something first? Water?

**LESLIE:**
No, I'm cool.

**KATIE:**
We were being kind of aggressive. We can be more caring.

**LESLIE:**
No no I don't need that.

**TRACY:**
You can have whatever you need.

**LESLIE:**
Are you all man-hating lesbians?
On the inside?

**KATIE:**
We're not lesbians.

**AMY:**
Sometimes I think I'm bisexual.

**DIANA:**
That's not the same. That's not the same as lesbian.
No one here is a lesbian.

**TRACY:**
We're not anti-lesbian for godsakes!

**LESLIE:**
It would be cool if you were.
Manhaters I mean.
I am.

**DIANA:**
Awesome.

**TRACY:**

Look maybe my story about free bleeding got us off on the wrong note. You can share as much as you feel comfortable. No pressure.

**LESLIE:**

Okay.

He said he wanted to feel small.

I don't want to give details. I'm... how do I explain?

I'm good at being in charge of sex. I take control. I boss guys around. Consensually.

I uh I spent a lot of time figuring out how to own that and do it well.

Usually they like it. But this time.

I don't know how it happened.

I wasn't in control anymore.

He just it he went too far and he hurt me and threatened me

and got really aggressive.

**TRACY:**

I'm so sorry

**DIANA:**

That's really fucked.

**LESLIE:**

That's.... I don't want to say anymore.

**KATIE:**

That's TOTALLY fine.

**TRACY:**

No one has to say any more than they want to.

**DIANA:**

Well I mean if you want to press charges you do.

**LESLIE:**
I don't.

**KATIE:**
Cool.

**TRACY:**
Do you want to have any other kind of response?

**LESLIE:**
Like what?

**DIANA:**
Well there's options.

**KATIE:**
Sure.  Sometimes we have a uh process.

**TRACY:**
Doesn't have to be whatever Diana said, it's always survivor-specific. Might involve us like reaching out to the guy?

**DIANA:**
Rapist.

**KATIE:**
Perpetrator.

**AMY:**
Person who perpetrated.

**TRACY:**
Yeah and like working with him

**AMY:**
Or her

**DIANA:**
Or them

**TRACY:**
To uh own what they did.  Really take responsibility.

**AMY:**
Accountability.

**DIANA:**
And then we might suggest next steps.

**LESLIE:**
Like what?

**AMY:**
Like that he joins the men's peer education group.

**TRACY:**
That's a group we work in partnership with.

**DIANA:**
It's like a space for men to confront all the shit they've internalized about taking up space and abusing women.

**KATIE:**
Okay what Di means is that it's a space for men to educate each other about male privilege and how to ask for consent.

**LESLIE:**
I know what it is.
He's in it.

**TRACY:**
Wait.

**KATIE:**
Seriously?

**DIANA:**
Who is it?

**AMY:**
She doesn't have to—

**LESLIE:**
I'm not gonna—

**KATIE:**
There's not that many people in it.

**DIANA:**
We like know them all.

*They look at each other.*

# Scene Six

*TRACY and JORDAN on a date.*

**TRACY:**

I'm not a free bleeder.

**JORDAN:**

It would be totally okay if you were.

**TRACY:**

I'm just interested in the movement. As a future OB--GYN.

**JORDAN:**

Pete shouldn't have been like that.

**TRACY:**

You don't have to apologize for him.

**JORDAN:**

He totally missed how he was interrupting you, and talking like an expert and I mean he's never menstruated! You know what I'm saying? He meant well but god.

**TRACY:**

You're not responsible for the whole patriarchy.

**JORDAN:**

Okay sure but I'm a part of it. And I'm sorry about when Adam tried to touch your hair without asking.

**TRACY:**

It's cool.

**JORDAN:**

I had a talk with him afterwards. I told him about entitlement to women's bodies, and exotification of black women, and colonization generally. He was really defensive but I think I got in there.

**TRACY:**

Cool. Did you find out about /Saturday night?

**JORDAN:**

Oh and I also wanted to apologize for my mom. She totally means well, she's just a middle-aged white Jewish lady so when she says "I've worked with lots of black people and I don't see them as any different" she's just trying to be nice. She doesn't have any context for how fucked that is /but I'm gonna break it down for her the next time we talk on the phone.

**TRACY:**

It's fine. It's really fine.

**JORDAN:**

It was awesome for her to meet you. She really loved it. She's so psyched you're gonna come home with me for Passover.

**TRACY:**

I am too.

**JORDAN:**

You're gonna meet my whole family.

**TRACY**

Wow.

**JORDAN:**

Damn my muscles are sore. Film thesis is essentially a gym membership. I should tell that to prospective majors.

**TRACY:**

Did you find out about your shoot Saturday night?

**JORDAN:**

It's a go. Only time we could get permission to be in the football field for four hours straight. And I'm up against a deadline. I really need that final scene to be in a recognizable stronghold of masculinity. We scouted the soccer field but it just wasn't the same, even the tennis courts looked a little wussy, I mean this film is about really UNDOING entitlement /so it has to be football.

**TRACY:**

I know what your thesis is about.

**JORDAN:**

I wish I could be with you that night.

**TRACY:**

Yeah I mean I have kinda been eating and breathing MCAT for the last YEAR so I did kinda think you were /gonna be with me the night I finished the big monster.

**JORDAN:**

I'm really sorry.

**TRACY:**

It's cool. I know your thesis is important.
You did kinda flinch when we were talking about it.
Free bleeding.

**JORDAN:**

Me? Flinch about /free bleeding?

**TRACY:**

Don't try to deny it.

**JORDAN:**

Well maybe I hadn't thought about it before.

**TRACY:**

So you did flinch.

**JORDAN:**

I don't know maybe but I'm over it now.
Free bleed away.

**TRACY:**

Are you
Are you into rough sex?

**JORDAN:**

What?

**TRACY:**

Like sex where you like beat each other up and stuff.
Consensually.

**JORDAN:**

Like bondage and domination stuff?
Is that something you want to try?

**TRACY:**
No! I just wanna know if you're into it.

**JORDAN:**
I uh... I mean I could be into it I would just need to learn /a little bit more—

**TRACY:**
Have you ever done it before?

**JORDAN:**
No I don't think so.

**TRACY:**
Are you sure?

**JORDAN:**
Um yeah pretty sure.

**TRACY:**
Do you know if any of the other guys in your group have tried it?

**JORDAN:**
Um no. We don't really talk about stuff like that.

**TRACY:**
Do you guys still do that thing where you get stuff off your chest?

**JORDAN:**
That's like our whole group. Guys getting stuff off of their chests.

**TRACY:**
What kinds of stuff do guys say?

**JORDAN:**
All kinds of stuff.

**TRACY:**

Like what?

**JORDAN:**

Everything you can think of.

**TRACY:**

What do you do when someone confesses really terrible stuff?

**JORDAN:**

Try to learn from it. Talk about how it could have gone differently. Try to be prepared for the next time.

**TRACY:**

Why don't you report it?

**JORDAN:**

No one's ever done something that was that terrible.

**TRACY:**

You said all kinds of stuff

**JORDAN:**

Not like worth reporting kind of stuff

**TRACY:**

What would that be?

**JORDAN:**

I mean you know.

**TRACY:**

So no one in the group has ever assaulted someone?

**JORDAN:**

I didn't say that.

**TRACY:**

Well then why don't you report the things?

**JORDAN:**

Those things typically happen before they join the group.

**TRACY:**

How do you know? When they confess it? How do you know it didn't happen last week?

**JORDAN:**

Well I think they would say.

**TRACY:**

Why do you think that?

**JORDAN:**

I don't know. Why are you being like this?

**TRACY:**

If someone in your group did something like assaulted someone and they confessed tomorrow in a meeting would you tell me?

**JORDAN:**

I probably would have to respect confidentiality.

**TRACY:**

Would you report it?

**JORDAN:**

Probably.

**TRACY:**

But you didn't report the other ones.

**JORDAN:**

What other ones?

**TRACY:**

You said people did terrible things.

**JORDAN:**

Did something happen?

Did you hear something?

**TRACY:**

I want to know what you would do.

**JORDAN:**

You're being a little

**TRACY:**

What?

**JORDAN:**

Extreme.

**TRACY:**

This isn't how I thought this would go.

**JORDAN:**

How did you think it would go?

**TRACY:**

I don't know.  I didn't think you'd be defensive.

**JORDAN:**

I'm being honest.

**TRACY:**

Sometimes you have a hard time receiving criticism.

**JORDAN:**

Well you're not giving it in a very nice way.  You should try using I statements and a friendlier tone of voice. That's the best way to get people to hear it. There've been studies on stuff like this. When you get aggressive people don't actually have a chance to learn.

*Pause.*

**JORDAN:**
You
You wanna go to dinner?
Hey.

**TRACY:**
I don't know.

**JORDAN:**
Are you okay?

**TRACY:**
I think I might need some time alone.

**JORDAN:**
Oh. Okay.
Well do you want to hang out later?

**TRACY:**
I don't know.
I might need some space.

**JORDAN:**
Space?

**TRACY:**
Like a break.

**JORDAN:**
Okay.
Okay.
You know I'm like one of the better boyfriends you can find out there. I'm working on my shit.

**TRACY:**
I thought we weren't saying boyfriend girlfriend yet.

**JORDAN:**
Well then what am I supposed to say?

**TRACY:**

We only started seeing each other a few months ago.

**JORDAN:**

That's eons in college time.

**TRACY:**

Well I guess I move slower than college time.

**JORDAN:**

I can slow down.

**TRACY:**

I'm not asking for a slowdown I'm asking for a break.

**JORDAN:**

What do you want me to do differently?

**TRACY:**

Jordan please.

**JORDAN:**

You like met my mom.

**TRACY:**

I think we both need a break.

**JORDAN:**

Wait seriously?
What am I gonna tell my mom?

**TRACY:**

That we're taking a break.

**JORDAN:**

She like LOVED you, she said she thinks you're the ONE.

**TRACY:**

I don't actually know what you should tell your mom.

**JORDAN:**

You were supposed to come home with me for Pass-over. And like my film friends I mean they thought I was gonna bring you to my thesis screening, can we get back together by then?

**TRACY:**

Maybe we'll talk in a few weeks.

**JORDAN:**

Would you come to the screening with me even if we're technically on a break?

**TRACY:**

I don't know.

**JORDAN:**

As friends.  Clearly.

**TRACY:**

I really can't say right now.

**JORDAN:**

You don't even want to be my friend?  After getting to know me?

**TRACY:**

I think a lot will make sense after we take some space.

**JORDAN:**

Was this even real for you?

**TRACY:**

I'm not gonna take care of your feelings! My god.

**JORDAN:**

I really thought I meant something to you.

**TRACY:**
I have to go now.

# Scene Seven

*Classroom.*

*Men's Peer Education Group.*

*The men all stand in a line.*

**TYLER:**
Raising your voice in conversation.

> *TYLER, PETE, DANNY, and JORDAN all step forward.*

> *They look at WILL.*

> *WILL steps forward.*

> *They all step back.*

**DANNY:**
Interrupting.

> *They all step forward.*

> *They all step back.*

**TYLER:**

Using statistics to make a point.

> *DANNY, TYLER and JORDAN step forward.*

> *DANNY, TYLER and JORDAN step back.*

**PETE:**

Putting your hands on girls.
Without asking.

> *They all step forward.*

> *They all step back.*

**DANNY:**

Telling a girl or woman to calm down.

> *They all step forward.*

> *They all step back.*

**TYLER:**

Asking a girl or woman to smile on the street.

> *TYLER, JORDAN and PETE step forward.*

> *TYLER, JORDAN and PETE step back.*

**PETE:**

Slapping a girl's ass.

> *He steps forward.*

> *So does WILL.*

> *PETE shakes his head or makes a noise at his frustra-*

*tion about DANNY, TYLER and JORDAN.*

*TYLER and DANNY step forward.*

*JORDAN does too.*

*They all step back.*

**PETE:**
Convincing her to have sex with you because you bought her a drink.

*He steps forward.*

*Long pause.*

*TYLER steps forward.*

*DANNY, WILL and JORDAN stay put.*

**PETE:**
You guys are liars.

**TYLER:**
Everyone self-reports.

*PETE steps back. So does TYLER.*

**DANNY:**
Ending sex after I came whether or not she did.

*They all step forward. They all step back.*

**PETE:**
Having sex with her after she said she didn't want to.

*PETE steps forward.*

*WILL steps forward.*

*Long Pause.*

*TYLER steps forward.*

*DANNY steps forward*

*JORDAN steps forward.*

*They all step back.*

**TYLER:**
I'm so glad you're here with us, Pete.

**DANNY:**
Me too.

**WILL:**
Are we all rapists?

**DANNY:**
Well, yes. We all did just admit to having participated in non-consensual sexual relations.

**WILL:**
I wasn't talking about forcing a girl I was talking about she said no and then like I convinced her.

**TYLER:**
Not all rape looks how it does on the news.

**DANNY:**
There's a spectrum of behavior.

**PETE:**
That's why we say rape CULTURE. Am I right guys, am I right?

**TYLER:**

Well what we're trying to promote is a culture of consent. Which is about hearing someone. I mean really hearing. Taking cues not just from what they say but how they act, how they behave. Yeah? That clear everyone?

Cool.

**DANNY:**

So the next thing we have to talk about is Jones.

**TYLER:**

Oh man Jones.

**PETE:**

Love Jones.

**WILL:**

Who's Jones?

**DANNY:**

Faculty advisor.

Grand midwife of men's peer education.

**PETE:**

That's weird man. Midwife? Nah.

**DANNY:**

Doula? My sister's a doula.

**PETE:**

Nah stop.

**TYLER:**

Maybe you're just being anti-woman.

**PETE:**

Maybe I don't think this thing is a baby.

**DANNY**

Anyway Jones is writing an article about our group. It's part of his tenure portfolio, he's citing being our faculty advisor as a pretty central part of his tenure case. So he's gonna be interviewing us. Starting with the founders, and then moving on to newer members. So these are consent forms. Take them home, think about it, and bring 'em back next week.[2]

**PETE:**

I wish Jones was my Dad.

**JORDAN:**

Uh—

**PETE:**

What?

**JORDAN:**

That's weird man.

**PETE:**

No it's not.

I mean I love my dad but he's so loud.

Always yelling at my mom.

And never got to have an important job like all of your dads.

So he never had that...

I don't know that confidence.

Just worked outside with power tools all day, people bossing him and stuff.

And that, that started to get to him.

But imagine having a dad like Jones! So quiet and

---

[2] For virtual productions this line can be changed to: "So you'll find consent forms in your email inbox. Think about it and sign 'em by next week."

smart and everything, so confident and careful and thoughtful about how to be around women and stuff. Then we'd all be different. We wouldn't even have to be here!

**JORDAN:**

I dunno about that.

**DANNY:**

I mean my dad was pretty quiet.

**JORDAN:**

Same.

**DANNY:**

And sure he had all kinds of power—big fancy company president and all. But he still did messed up shit. Still interrupted and talked over my mom and sister. I'm still trying hard not to become him.

**PETE:**

That's deep man. Thanks for sharing that.

**DANNY**

No problem.

**TYLER:**

And like, Jones isn't our Dad he's our Jones!

**WILL:**

Hey guys?
I wanna tell you guys something.

**PETE:**

Bring it on, man.

**WILL:**

Okay.
Okay so.

I had a dream last night.
Real weird one.
In the dream this uh stuff was staining my pants. It's
hard to explain. I looked down and my crotch was
all red and I thought geez what's going on, and it was
spreading quickly and then I realized: this was my period and I was free bleeding. That thing we were talking
about. It was happening to me. It was terrifying. I
woke up screaming.

**PETE:**
Whoa man.

**DANNY:**
What a dream.

**TYLER:**
What do you think it means?

**WILL:**
I'm afraid of women. Their power. You all know what
I'm talking about.
Their dark, mysterious power. That thing they have. It
makes you want to impress them. Sometimes I think
they're a different species from us.

**PETE:**
I've thought that before too man.

**JORDAN:**
Oh-kay.

**PETE:**
I'm not saying that's true.
I'm just saying it's something I've thought.
You probably have too.
Right Jordan?

**JORDAN:**

I don't know about—

**PETE:**

He won't say it but he has.

**JORDAN:**

That is not what I said.

**PETE:**

You try to pretend you're so much better but you're no better than any of us.

**TYLER:**

Hey, man.

**DANNY:**

We do not compare ourselves in here.

**PETE:**

I wasn't comparing. I was saying we're all the same.

**DANNY:**

That's exactly what comparing is.

**WILL:**

Did you know that your cat would kill you if it could?

**PETE:**

I don't have a cat.

**WILL:**

All cats would kill their owners. If they could.

**TYLER:**

/What does this have to do with anything?

**DANNY:**

What do you mean if they could?

**WILL:**

If the circumstances were right. If the owners didn't fight back.

**TYLER:**

How does anyone know that?

**WILL:**

They've done studies.

**JORDAN:**

Who're they?

**PETE:**

What makes them think all cats are the same?

**WILL:**

That's just what studies have shown.

**JORDAN:**

I have a scenario. Scenario time? Let's say it's time for a scenario.

**DANNY:**

It's really time for a scenario.

**JORDAN:**

Okay so.

You're on a date with your girlfriend.

Let's say you love her.

Let's say you've been dating for few months.

Let's say just last weekend you and her went to dinner with your mother and your mother said, I can tell she's the one and called all your aunts and uncles and grandparents and told them you had met The One.

Then, let's say she stops trusting you.

You can't pinpoint it on any one thing you said or did.

She just stops trusting you.
She doesn't believe you anymore.
She doesn't think you're good.
To her you're just a man.
An ugly stupid useless no good white man.
You'll never unlearn dominance.
You'll never stop talking with too much authority or taking up too much space. You're just a man. And that means you're a lesser being. And she's probably going to turn into a lesbian now or something.
What do you do then?

**TYLER:**

Is this hypothetical?

**JORDAN:**

It's a scenario.

**DANNY:**

It's a new kind of scenario.

**JORDAN:**

C'mon man do the thing.

**DANNY:**

Most of our scenarios have to do with how to prevent sexual assault.

**JORDAN:**

It matters in relationships too. Most sexual assault happens between intimate partners.

**TYLER:**

Yup yup. True story.

**DANNY:**

It's just not the focus of our group.

**JORDAN:**
Everything is the focus of our group.

**WILL:**
You could apologize.

*They all look at him.*

**PETE:**
For what?

**WILL:**
For how you behaved.

**TYLER:**
That's a great start.

**JORDAN:**
But you didn't do just one thing.
That was part of the scenario.

**WILL:**
Well there must have been something.

**JORDAN:**
There wasn't.

**WILL:**
Did you ask her?

**TYLER:**
It's hypothetical.

**JORDAN:**
She's not getting mad at YOU she's getting mad at
the idea of you. The idea of how horrible men can
be. She's blind/ to the fact that you're one of the good
ones-

**DANNY:**

Ouch.

**JORDAN:**

What the fuck man

**DANNY:**

Able-ist language. Blind to.

**JORDAN:**

Well what am I supposed to say?

**DANNY:**

I don't know. What are you trying to say?

**JORDAN:**

That she was fucking blind to it!

**DANNY:**

Blind people aren't oblivious to everything in the world.

**JORDAN:**

I'm trying to say that she
LITERALLY DIDN'T SEE ME
OR all the hard fucking work that I was putting into being with her like skipping film shoots to go to meetings and reading feminism books instead of watching movies it was fucking hundreds of hours I put into this whole gig. It doesn't come easy to be a sensitive guy you got to earn that shit and I did. And she didn't see that. And there is no other word for that other than blind. That is what blind means. It means you don't see. She didn't see.

**TYLER:**

Oh man.

**PETE:**
Dude.

**DANNY:**
That blows man.

**PETE:**
Everything you been through.

**TYLER:**
Break-ups are the worst.

**DANNY:**
I am so sorry. I really am.

**PETE:**
Was it last night?

**JORDAN:**
It's just a scenario.

**DANNY:**
Okay so the blind thing /is like

**JORDAN:**
Don't fucking correct my language.

**WILL:**
I thought you said it was a long road.

**JORDAN:**
What are you fucking talking about?

**TYLER:**
Hey man don't be like that with him.

**PETE:**
Yeah let's be cool.

**JORDAN:**

Now you're all gonna jump on me, huh?

**DANNY:**

No no we're just trying to enforce respect.

**WILL:**

You said that last time. It's a long road. To getting over male privilege.

**JORDAN:**

That is not at all what we are talking about here. We are talking about scared blind pissy little girls. Who are too wimpy to handle the greater world and everything in it which includes bad guys and good guys and sensitive guys and sometimes the good ones remind you of the bad ones but you gotta fucking get over that because you can't live your whole life cutting out half of the species. You just can't.

**PETE:**

Less than half.

*JORDAN glares at Pete.*

Well men are actually a little bit less than half.

**JORDAN:**

What the fuck, man?

**PETE:**

They are.

**TYLER:**

It seems like you're dealing with some stuff today. Like you might need to step out and take a break.

**JORDAN:**

I'll decide when I need to take a break.

**DANNY:**
Maybe we should end the meeting for the day.

**PETE:**
Sounds like a good call.

**WILL:**
Are we gonna do the /cheer thing?

**DANNY:**
Not this time.

**PETE:**
See you all next week! Hope you can work it out with her Jordan!

*He exits.*

**JORDAN:**
Fuck you.

**WILL:**
See you...guys...?
Okay whatever.

*He exits.*

**DANNY:**
What the...?

**TYLER:**
Jordan, man.

**JORDAN:**
You know Pete said sex without consent and we all stepped forward.

**TYLER:**
Well sure.

**JORDAN:**

And we're not gonna report any of those rapes? Not even gonna ask about them?

**DANNY:**

We stepped forward because we're learning how to be better and we have to acknowledge how we've messed up until now.

**JORDAN:**

Up until when? Up until last night? Were we stepping forward cuz we raped a girl two years ago or cuz we raped her an hour ago?

**DANNY:**

I can tell that breaking up with Tracy did a number on you. I mean I remember when Theresa and I split it was like—

**JORDAN:**

How do we know we're any different from the frat houses or the football team? Getting together after practice being like, did you get some this weekend? Huh? Oh great, and as soon as you deal with your guilt about it you can go out and do it again!

**TYLER:**

We don't congratulate each other!

**JORDAN:**

Someone here fucked up and I lost the best girlfriend in the world.

**TYLER:**

/What do you mean someone fucked up?

**DANNY:**

What happened with Tracy that is really /fucked man
I'm so sorry—

**JORDAN:**

We all fucked up. As long as we're all lying everything
about this group is a joke. We might as well disband.

**TYLER:**

We're not all lying.

**DANNY:**

I'm gonna ask you to take some time.
Don't you think that's best, Tyler?

**TYLER:**

Yup. I agree. I mean you're bringing real critiques man
I think we should talk about them, but constructively.
When you're ready for that.

**DANNY:**

You hear what we're saying, man?  It's for your own
sake.
You take a break. You get yourself together. You decide
when it's time to come back.

# Scene Eight

*TYLER and LESLIE.*

**LESLIE:**
How come you have keys to this room?

**TYLER:**
I run a student group that meets here.

**LESLIE:**
Which one?

**TYLER:**
I'd like to keep that confidential.

**LESLIE:**
I sort of joined a group that meets here too.

**TYLER:**
That's great.

**LESLIE:**
Is this your first creative writing class?

**TYLER:**
My story's that bad, huh?

**LESLIE:**

No! I was just like trying to get to know you.

**TYLER:**

I'm a senior concentrator. My thesis is a novel. Marcus is my advisor. Which is probably why I don't talk that much in class—I've had her workshop twice already so I try to give new peeps a chance. And I think prolly why she matched us up for critique. She likes to pair students with different levels of experience. It's a specific pedagogy thing.

**LESLIE:**

What's it about?

**TYLER:**

My thesis? It's three generations of one family. Black family moving from a rural landscape to a big city.

**LESLIE:**

Autobiographical?

**TYLER:**

Man. Just cuz I'm mixed doesn't mean everything I write about black people is autobiographical.

**LESLIE:**

Sorry. Sorry sorry.

**TYLER:**

I mean is everything in your story true? Are you running a dominatrix service out of your dorm room?

**LESLIE:**

No! I mean I'm sorry.
She's not actually running a dominatrix service. She's just dominating that guy. It's consensual power play.

No one's paying.

**TYLER:**

Ohh-kay.

**LESLIE:**

Let's just do the thing.

**TYLER:**

You wanna start or should I?

**LESLIE:**

I mean you probably don't wanna hear anything I have to say about your story. Cuz you're like a senior concentrator and this is my first creative writing class.

**TYLER:**

I deserve to get feedback on my work the same way you do.

**LESLIE:**

Okay, alright. Well to be honest I thought the sister character was kind of quiet. Like her brother gets all the air time at family dinner.

**TYLER:**

That's realistic.

**LESLIE:**

It's also fucked up.

**TYLER:**

Yeah but that's how it would happen.

**LESLIE:**

You shouldn't let your story be fucked up because it's realistic.

**TYLER:**

That's one of the main roles of the writer. In my view. Reveal fucked up shit about society.

**LESLIE:**

It didn't really seem like you were doing it on purpose. I mean the sister character just seemed dumb and shallow the whole story long. She never really got any depth.

**TYLER:**

Oooh-kay.

**LESLIE:**

Was that too harsh?

**TYLER:**

Not at all. I can totally take it.

**LESLIE:**

Do you have any questions?

**TYLER:**

I think I'm good.

**LESLIE:**

Sorry.

**TYLER:**

Don't apologize.

**LESLIE:**

Okay.

**TYLER:**

Should we switch over?

**LESLIE:**

Are you ready for that? I mean I didn't really /give you

that much.

**TYLER:**

I'm good.

**LESLIE:**

Cool well whaddaya got for me?

**TYLER:**

Well this felt fresh. I haven't read a story like this before, honestly. And I read a lot. I really appreciated the way you were naming the guy's male privilege. The way he takes up space and mainsplains and stuff. I think it was cool that you included that word: mansplaining. That you had the girl call him out. I mean woman.

**LESLIE:**

Thanks.

**TYLER:**

And my main reaction was... okay so the thing that happens....

**LESLIE:**

The assault?

**TYLER:**

Well yeah that was actually what I wanted to talk about. It's kind of fuzzy what happens.

**LESLIE:**

What do you mean?

**TYLER:**

Well I get that he crosses a boundary while she's beating him up, I mean definitely, he is DEFINITELY not entitled to touch her that way or do that to her, but it seems like she kind of taunts him.

**LESLIE:**

I mean she's a dom. She's trying to stay in control.

**TYLER:**

Right okay. I guess what I mean is I didn't think it was realistic that a guy who was educated enough about his privilege to name misogyny and mansplaining and stuff would let himself get so aggressive with her. He even talks about the group he's in! I think it's not realistic that he would like push her up against the wall and hold her down and stuff. You know what I mean? That part really stood out to me. See I wrote— "I don't believe this," in the margins. It's kind of an inconsistent character.

**LESLIE:**

What's inconsistent about that?

**TYLER:**

I mean if he went there to get beat up by her I don't know if he would order her around and tell her to just do what he says. That really broke with the consistency for me.

**LESLIE:**

Okay.

**TYLER:**

And I REALLY don't think he would take her phone and keep her from calling campus security. That part's super hard to believe. Or that he would make it all about him. The way that he bullies her into not reporting it because it would ruin HIS future. You know what I'm talking about? This part on page five:

"I already got into Law School, I'm about to graduate, you would be taking my future away from me..."
I don't know. I just think he would have some more consciousness at some point. Especially since it seems like he's working on his shit. I think you should be nicer to the character. He really comes off as an asshole and not ALL men suck, am I right? Overall it just kind of lacked believability.
Y'know what I mean?
Are you... okay?

# Scene Nine

*Meeting.*

*Survivor Support Group.*

*They sit in a circle.*

*AMY stands, holding a rock.*

**AMY:**
He comes to everything I do.
The vegan working group of
the Improving Campus Dining Collective The
Asian-American Student Union1. Parties at my dorm.
My English class.
Seriously.
He transferred in at the THIRD CLASS After the
add-drop period was over.
Like he was stalking me.
He wasn't stalking me though.
He seemed not to remember me.
Not to remember my name.
For the record I wasn't wearing a short skirt. I wasn't
wearing makeup.

I wasn't wearing a low-cut top.
I was in my gym clothes.
My favorite sweat pants.
That I never wear anymore.
And I was sweaty and stinky.
And sitting on a couch in the hockey team common
room.
And now I don't go back to that room.
And I don't put on those pants.
I keep them in my closet, though.
Folded on a hanger
between clothes I do wear.
Sometimes I touch them by accident.
When I reach for something else.
And then I notice them
twisting back and forth.

*She sits back down.*

*She passes the rock to KATIE.*

**KATIE:**

Sometimes I have dreams about the room. The window
blinds. The marks on the floor. The whir of the fan. I
can't go in when I go home. Thank god we don't use it
for anything anymore. Doesn't matter how many years
go by. I shake when I walk through the doorway.
And then I cry in the shower.

*She passes the rock to DIANA.*

**DIANA:**

I noticed this guy at the library trying to look down my shirt. So then I was like okay I guess I won't wear that shirt anymore. And then this weekend I was getting dressed to go out. And I didn't know what to wear. Suddenly it was like none of my shirts were safe. I tried on five different outfits. None of my favorite dresses are okay anymore. None of my skirts or tight jeans. Finally I was back in my pajamas sitting on my bed.
The better I look the less safe I feel.

*DIANA passes the rock to TRACY.*

**TRACY:**

I went to see my T.A. to get help studying for my organic chemistry final and he was DEFINITELY checking me out in a super sleazy way for the first five minutes. And then he kept being like, oh wow, oh you're really smart, and stuff like he was so surprised that I had learned a thing or two about organic chemistry and then at the end he was like you know you might be med school material. And I was like fuck you guess who just finished the MCATS this weekend and then he proceeded to talk my ear off for about ten minutes of patronizing-as-fuck-shit about women and people of color in medicine and how much easier it is for us to get into medical school because there's something "special" about us and how it would be so much harder for him as one of a billion white guys.

*They all groan.*

*TRACY passes the stone to LESLIE*

**LESLIE:**
Well. It's only my second time.
I don't know.

**TRACY:**
Can be any kind of grievance.

**LESLIE:**
Okay well I was thinking about how since the guy was in the men's peer education group when it happened, silence about this is like just even more disgusting. It just means they can keep assaulting people and going back to their group and then what? Nothing happens? So I think I want to say something. That's what I think I want now.

**TRACY:**
Okay with everyone if I break the activity?

*They nod.*

Okay. If reporting it would help you feel closure or move towards justice you should absolutely report it.

**DIANA:**
Agreed. We prefer not to go to the police unless you really want to.
We can report to the school. But they don't ever really do anything.

**LESLIE:**
What do you mean?

**DIANA:**
Didn't do shit for me.

**AMY:**
Or me.

**TRACY:**

Same same.  Unfortunately.

**KATIE:**

Mine happened before I got here so I didn't try to report it to them.

I mean they'll refer you to counseling.

**DIANA:**

With a counselor who might not believe you.

**TRACY:**

It's not very many sessions. I found the peer support was stronger.

**LESLIE:**

Why don't they do anything though?

**AMY:**

They want everything to be really black and white, clear, provable before they do anything.

**KATIE:**

That's pretty hard on survivors.

**DIANA**:

Also they don't care about us.

**TRACY:**

They do, they just care more about their image.  It doesn't look good for them if a student is a rapist.

**DIANA:**

Also they're afraid of being sued. Cuz they've gotten sued for defamation before. By a rapist.

**LESLIE:**

Yeah but don't they like care if we... I mean they must want us to have a good experience here?  Like doesn't that affect their image badly?  If we drop out?

**DIANA:**
They don't care if we drop out. Remember when Jessica dropped out and we tried to use it against them? They don't actually need our tuition.
If we go it's just a spot for someone else.

**LESLIE:**
Wow.

**DIANA:**
Yeah.

**AMY:**
Depressing.

**LESLIE:**
That's just. Damn.

**TRACY:**
But if reporting it would help you feel closure we can absolutely report it.

**LESLIE:**
What about direct action. Do you guys ever do that?
We did that in the anti-war group y'know we had that sit-in?

**KATIE:**
Like what Emma Sulkowicz at Columbia did?  How she carried around her
mattress?

**AMY:**
Men's Peer Education group HATES it when we talk about her.

**KATIE:**

An action could definitely get us disciplinary action.

**DIANA:**

That doesn't mean we shouldn't do it.

**TRACY:**

But we should make sure it's worth it.

That whatever we do means we get heard.

By whoever it is we want to hear us.

**AMY:**

It's the school, right? We want the whole school to hear us? We want them to know that the men's peer education group are rapists?

**KATIE:**

Well one of them. Not ALL.

**DIANA:**

Well they all let a rape happen.

**KATIE:**

Yeah but only one of them actually did it.

**DIANA:**

Well then the rest of them should have educated that one guy better.

**TRACY:**

I think we can hold the perpetrator accountable without attacking the whole group. I mean what if one of us did something and someone blamed all of us?

**AMY:**

It would be different cuz we're not guys.

**TRACY:**

We know that anyone can be a perpetrator.

**KATIE:**

Don't you think it's a little self-sabotaging? I mean we're in a coalition with them. Don't you think we should come to them directly with any issues?

**DIANA:**

I think we should focus on centering survivors' wishes.

**KATIE:**

How will this look to the admissions office—remember how we have to show them our new presentation next week and what are they gonna think of us if we do this?

**DIANA:**

Oh my god why are we letting the administration dictate what we do?

**KATIE:**

I just think we should try to maintain a positive relationship with a group we have to work with on a regular basis.

**AMY:**

Positive relationship is overrated.

**DIANA:**

We already have shit with them. It already sucks to lead trainings with them. You know how much space they take up. And they never stay for cleanup.

**AMY:**

Yeah NOT naming it would be passive aggressive.

**TRACY:**

Well I mean if we have shit with them and want to approach them that's a separate issue from wanting to call out Leslie's rapist.

Leslie, who's the target of this action? Is it the one guy? Or is it the men's peer education group? Or is it the whole school?

**LESLIE:**

I want the administration to get the message too. They're the ones that enable this. I mean especially if they don't do anything when you report incidents. Don't you think they'd wanna hear that this thing they are funding that is supposed to be preventing sexual assault is actually like... allowing it? And maybe a direct action would get their attention.

What if we get our parents to call in?

**DIANA:**

Didn't work for me. But we could try again.

**LESLIE:**

What if we get the professors on our side?

**TRACY:**

In the past it was challenging but we can certainly try. They've signed letters anonymously before.

**KATIE:**

There's a lot of competition for those jobs.

**LESLIE:**

Seems like they don't really care about anyone. Like who do they have to answer to? If it's not us and not our parents and not our professors like.... Who do they actually have to answer to?

**TRACY:**

Applicants. Prospective students. That's actually the only group they care about.

**DIANA:**

The most important thing is keeping their ranking high. Their status competitive. So of course the only people they care about are applicants.

**AMY:**

That's why the only time they care about us is when we're making a dumb presentation for prospective students.

**LESLIE:**

Maybe it doesn't have to be dumb.

**DIANA:**

What?

**LESLIE:**

I mean, presenting for prospective students
That might actually be the only chance we have to get the school to hear us.
Maybe we have a different kind of presentation to make.

# Scene Ten

*Men's Peer Education Group. Everyone except JOR-DAN.*

*They stand in a line.*

**PETE:**
Thinking you might be smarter than a girl.
Just cuz you're a guy.

> *WILL steps forward.*

> *TYLER and DANNY do too.*

> *DANNY steps forward.*

**DANNY:**
Thinking you know what's best for a woman.

> *All others step forward.*

> *They all step back.*

**DANNY:**
Trying to make it seem like you're different from other men because of the music you listen to or the food you

eat or the way you talk.

*He steps forward.*

*TYLER steps forward.*

*They step back.*

*PETE steps forward.*

**PETE:**
Wishing you were a woman. Not because you're like a transsexual just cuz you want to be done with guilt and shame.
Oh c'mon, nobody's with me?
Will man you had that dream.

**DANNY:**
We don't call others out.

*WILL steps forward.*

*So does TYLER.*

*So does DANNY.*

*They all step back.*

*PETE steps forward.*

**PETE:**
Thinking girls are ugly. Especially fat ones. Or acne covered ones.
Thinking they should lose weight or learn how to apply makeup.

*WILL steps forward.*

*So does TYLER*

*So does DANNY.*

*WILL steps forward.*

**WILL:**
Thinking she's a BITCH when she's on her cycle.

*The others step forward.*

*They all step back.*

*TYLER steps forward.*

**TYLER:**
Not stopping when she says no.

*WILL steps forward.*

*Then PETE.*

*They wait.*

*They all step back.*

**TYLER:**
Not stopping when she says no the second time.

*He steps forward.*

*WILL and PETE step forward.*

*They all step back.*

**TYLER:**
Telling her not to report it because no one will believe

her.

*He steps forward.*

Telling her reporting it would be taking away your future.
Telling her you already got into law school.

**DANNY:**
What's going on, Man?

**TYLER:**
Threatening to do something to her if she tells.
Thinking you're teaching her a lesson.
Thinking you're putting her in her place.

**DANNY:**
What the fuck are you doing?

**TYLER:**
Do you have something to say?
Do you have something to tell us, man?

**PETE:**
What's going on?

**TYLER:**
That's exactly what I wanna ask Danny.

**WILL:**
Is there something going on? Guys?

**PETE:**
Is this about Jordan? Is this why he's not here?

**TYLER:**
Someone here's lying and maybe we all are.
I'm done.
Y'all can decide what to do.

*He leaves.*

**PETE:**
What the fuck first Jordan, now Tyler?
Tyler's my model, man.

**DANNY:**
I know.

**PETE:**
If Tyler's out I'm out.

**DANNY:**
No one's *out* okay—

**PETE:**
Sure seems like Jordan was. Sure seems like Tyler is.

**DANNY:**
He'll be back.

**WILL:**
Is this meeting over? Cuz I have soccer.

**DANNY:**
Do what you gotta do.

**PETE:**
Well are we meeting next week?

**DANNY:**
I don't know.
I really don't know.

**PETE:**
Shit, man.

> *PETE leaves.*

> *WILL starts to leave and then stops.*

**WILL:**

Did something happen with someone?
Danny?
Did someone do something?

> *WILL waits a minute and then leaves.*

> *DANNY's alone.*

# Scene Eleven

*DANNY and JONES.*

*The classroom.*

**JONES:**
So start by stating your name.

**DANNY:**
Are you gonna use my real name?

**JONES:**
I don't have to.
Do you want me not to?

**DANNY:**
Yeah I would prefer you didn't.

**JONES:**
Alright then, don't say your name say Subject Number 1.

**DANNY:**
I'm your first subject?

**JONES:**
You're the founder.

**DANNY:**

One of.

**JONES:**

The first one who came to me with this idea and set it all into motion.

**DANNY:**

Well I don't know if—

**JONES:**

Don't be modest.

**DANNY:**

Let's just do the interview.

**JONES:**

Okay so first of all. What would you say is the main mission of the group?

**DANNY:**

Just—

**JONES:**

Yeah?

**DANNY:**

Where is this gonna go?

**JONES:**

Where is what gonna go?

**DANNY:**

The paper you're writing. I mean separate from your tenure portfolio. Where are you gonna publish it?

**JONES:**

Oh well we don't know yet. But I have a feeling some of the fancier publications are going to be pretty interesed. This is a pretty unique story.

**DANNY:**

There's groups like this at other schools.

**JONES:**

Not really.

Not like THIS.

**DANNY:**

What's unique about us?

**JONES:**

Well student-initiated first of all.

That day when you came in here and said to me—

**DANNY:**

That's going in the paper?

**JONES:**

That's the opener!

**DANNY:**

You already wrote it?

**JONES:**

Ahhem.

It was a crisp September morning when I heard the knock on my door. A freshman student from my Gender Politics in America seminar had come to see me with a very important question. The student came from a family line traceable to the Mayflower. He had been groomed for Watson with boarding school and tutors and private tennis lessons. His own father had endowed an athletic field. His question: How do I not become my father? This was the question that would change everything.

**DANNY:**
No way.

**JONES:**
Yup. That is the beginning.

**DANNY:**
Wow.

**JONES:**
I'll change your name obviously. Unless you don't want it changed.

**DANNY:**
You really think my question changed everything?

**JONES:**
Of course I do, I know your question changed every-thing.
Just look at all that's happened at the school because of it.

**DANNY:**
Right yeah.

**JONES:**
You know what happens when I bring up this group at conferences? When I talk about how at Watson we have a Men's Peer Education Group! Where students edu-cate each OTHER about male privilege and they work WITH the survivor support group. You should be very proud of your work.

**DANNY:**
I am. I am. A question though.

**JONES:**
Yes. Any question for you.

**DANNY:**

If the group is um.

If let's say something happened.

That someone in the group messed up.

Would that change this?

Like your paper and everything.

Would that change like...

Would the group not count anymore?

**JONES:**

I'm sure everyone in the group has messed up at some point. And that's why your group is so wonderful! People have it to go back to. After they mess up.

**DANNY:**

Right right. Okay. Okay.

But what if um—

**JONES:**

Is something wrong?

**DANNY:**

No, it's just that

Someone left our group. And then someone else left.

Because someone in our group did something

Really bad.

The kind of thing we're trying to get everyone everywhere not to do anymore. Someone in our group did that kind of thing.

**JONES:**

Well. People mess up.

You know that right?

**DANNY:**

Yes of course.

**JONES:**
That was always gonna be part of the deal with this group.
People unlearning privilege? They mess up all the time! The media's still giving them all of these messages about what it means to be a man, how to take power, dominate women, it's hard to turn off to all that. People fall into old patterns. And the really courageous, remarkable thing about all of you is that you're willing to confront that.

**DANNY:**
Right right. People mess up.
And then they learn from it.

**JONES:**
Exactly.

**DANNY:**
But what if it wasn't just anyone.
Like what if
what if
it was me?
I'm one of the founders, one of the leaders.
What would you say if I came to you and I said
I said I think I might have assaulted someone?

**JONES:**
Well. I would say.
I cannot condone what happened, what's been done.
But I know you.
And I know you as Danny
The one who came to me the first semester of your freshman year
And that Danny.

That Danny is still there.

That Danny is still inside you.

**DANNY:**

What

what would you say that person should do?

**JONES:**

I think you should get in there and respond to this thing! Whatever happened. Unpack it and figure out how it happened and how to not have it happen again! That's what this space is for. That's how this group is special.

**DANNY:**

So you uh

you don't think anyone should troop over to public safety or anything like that?

**JONES:**

No. No I don't. We need the group to continue. And you don't know what could happen after you do something like that—your future could change a lot. Legal battles, grad school, jobs... all of that could be affected. You can't afford to sabotage your future—you're going to be a lawyer! We need you out there!

Danny you haven't created something perfect but you've created something powerful. Wait 'til you read my article. I think you'll feel proud.

# Scene Twelve

*DIANA and PETE. Classroom.*

**PETE:**
You came!!

**DIANA:**
Yeah.

**PETE:**
I was so worried you wouldn't come. Thanks so much for meeting. I know it's kind of weird. I really love your music more than anything else; that's what prompted this. I mean your last piece at the open mic about the stain on the wall—it's also the last song on your album? Just beautiful.

**DIANA:**
Cool.

**PETE:**
The part about if the stain could move—if the stain could cry but it's stuck there? That was just beautiful. As a poet I was inspired by your art.

**DIANA:**
Neat.

**PETE:**

Are you like annoyed?

**DIANA:**

What?

**PETE:**

You just like seem annoyed. I'm like trying to talk to you about your music and you only have one-word responses.

**DIANA:**

What do you want an essay?

**PETE:**

I thought artist to artist we might be able to connect.

**DIANA:**

Oh right. You're not exactly my audience.

**PETE:**

Wh-what do you mean by that?
I am your audience—I love your work.

**DIANA:**

Oh my god. You know why I did NOT write that song? So that GUYS could tell me my song about survivor-hood was beautiful.

**PETE:**

It was though.

**DIANA:**

If I could make my shows a women's only space I would.

**PETE:**

Well I didn't know it was about survivor-hood.

**DIANA:**

Yeah see this is what I was talking about.
Not the audience.

**PETE:**

I didn't. I mean it makes sense since so many of your
other songs directly reference assault, I mean your
whole album does. I really see how that song fits into it
now. Man, it's really great for me to get to talk to you
and know a little bit more about the woman behind the
work! The survivor behind the work.
Did I say something wrong?

**DIANA:**

That song is not for you.
I'm not some perfect pretty survivor making nice music
so that you think rape isn't actually that bad. I'm gonna
be angry and messy and ugly and call out every fucking
man who is complicit in our rape culture.

**PETE:**

Wow. Thanks for sharing that with me.

**DIANA:**

No problem.

**PETE:**

The song did feel messy to me. That's what I liked
about it.
I'm not a survivor. But my aunt is.
Got raped in a detention center. Took so much time
and money for us just to get her out of there and it
wasn't 'til afterwards that she told us about all the
abuse. She said the staff made her sign something
stating her rape was consensual but it wasn't. It really
wasn't. She got harassed nonstop. And anyway she was

a big reason I joined the men's peer education group.
Really important space for me.
I shared your song with her. Your whole album actual-
ly. She loved it.
She actually asked me if I could get your autograph.
That was part of why I kept pushing you to meet.

**DIANA:**
Oh. Geez. I'm sorry I was so flaky.
I mean I can autograph... I'm not like famous or any-
thing.

**PETE:**
It would make her really happy.

**DIANA:**
Okay. Okay cool. I'll write her a little note. What's
her name?

**PETE:**
Cynthia. Or you can say Cyndi.

**DIANA:**
Cyndi.

*She takes a while.*

Here you go.

**PETE:**
Oh man she's gonna love it and her birthday's next
week.

**DIANA:**
Did um anything ever happen? For her?

**PETE:**
Huh?

**DIANA:**

Like did the detention center ever acknowledge that she was raped?

**PETE:**

Oh. No. No way. They can't admit that rape happens there. They'd get in too much trouble.

**DIANA:**

Right.
Kinda like here.

**PETE:**

Hah, yeah. Kinda like here.

**DIANA:**

Can I ask you something about the group? Do you think you've like gotten anything out of it?

**PETE:**

You kidding? Men's Peer Education Group saved my life. I don't know who I'd be without it.
But you know something else I've been thinking?
We didn't go far enough. Our group was.... it wasn't enough. There was more we could've done. More we could've asked. Of ourselves. Of each other. That's why it fell apart in the end. We didn't go far enough. I'm thinking about starting a new group. I got some ideas.

# Scene Thirteen

*Classroom. Admissions Officer projects an image of a dead white guy.*

**ADMISSIONS OFFICER:**
This is James Watson.
Founder of our college. Military man.
Grew up fighting in the Union Army. Battle of Gettysburg.
A courageous fellow, he stayed in the fight even when it wasn't easy.

> *As she is speaking members of the SURVIVOR SUP-PORT GROUP walk among the audience passing out flyers that say "Rape Happens Here," and "Do You Want a Rapist for Your RA?" And "How Watson Protects Rapists."*

He wrote letters home to his dear wife about how much he dreamed of founding a school for her to teach in. She was a history teacher who taught rooms full of illiterate children
in one-room schoolhouses covered by snow. Her dream was to—
excuse me. Excuse me! Girls!

**AMY:**

This is an important handout.[3]

**ADMISSIONS OFFICER:**

Well I'd like to kindly ask you to wait until I'm finished.

Where was I? So James Watson's wife Mary had a dream. And her dream was to start a college where the children could stay and learn in peace unhampered by the difficulties of rural life. And so James suffered through the long war. And all the while he wrote letters home to Mary. And when he finally got home he used everything he had to found a college for her to teach in. Right here. I'm sure it's clear to you that this is no ordinary school. This is a place where people take action. This is a place where dreams are realized, just as James Watson realized Mary's dream. This is a place where the impossible becomes possible. I invite you to realize your dreams at Watson College.

Now as part of your info-session today you'll be hearing from a graduating student, and a member of our student coalition to prevent sexual assault. Just one of the small ways that Watson is special.

*DANNY enters.*

**DANNY:**

Hi. Hi Everyone. I'm Danny and I'm pleased to be here today representing the most phenomenal institution on the planet and, quite honestly, the best four years of my life. An education that set me up to realize my dream. To become a lawyer. What I'm here to talk

---

[3] For virtual productions this line can be changed to "This is an important message."

about today is consent on our campus.

**TRACY:**

Rape happens here. Rape happens here.

**AMY:**

/Rape happens here.

**TRACY and AMY and KATIE:**

Rape happens here.
Rape happens here!
Rape happens here!
Rape happens here!

> *Their chanting grows louder and louder. It sounds like a thousand people chanting. ADMISSIONS encourages DANNY to keep speaking but he doesn't.*

> *END OF PLAY.*